Andromache by Euripides

Euripides is rightly lauded as one of the great dramatists of all time. In his lifetime, he wrote over 90 plays and although only 18 have survived they reveal the scope and reach of his genius.

Euripides is identified with many theatrical innovations that have influenced drama all the way down to modern times, especially in the representation of traditional, mythical heroes as ordinary people in extraordinary circumstances.

As would be expected from a life lived 2,500 years ago, details of it are few and far between. Accounts of his life, written down the ages, do exist but whether much is reliable or surmised is open to debate.

Most accounts agree that he was born on Salamis Island around 480 BC, to mother Cleito and father Mnesarchus, a retailer who lived in a village near Athens. Upon the receipt of an oracle saying that his son was fated to win "crowns of victory", Mnesarchus insisted that the boy should train for a career in athletics.

However, what is clear is that athletics was not to be the way to win crowns of victory. Euripides had been lucky enough to have been born in the era as the other two masters of Greek Tragedy; Sophocles and Æschylus. It was in their footsteps that he was destined to follow.

His first play was performed some thirteen years after the first of Socrates plays and a mere three years after Æschylus had written his classic The Oristria.

Theatre was becoming a very important part of the Greek culture. The Dionysia, held annually, was the most important festival of theatre and second only to the fore-runner of the Olympic games, the Panathenia, held every four years, in appeal.

Euripides first competed in the City Dionysia, in 455 BC, one year after the death of Æschylus, and, incredibly, it was not until 441 BC that he won first prize. His final competition in Athens was in 408 BC. The Bacchae and Iphigenia in Aulis were performed after his death in 405 BC and first prize was awarded posthumously. Altogether his plays won first prize only five times.

Euripides was also a great lyric poet. In Medea, for example, he composed for his city, Athens, "the noblest of her songs of praise". His lyric skills however are not just confined to individual poems: "A play of Euripides is a musical whole....one song echoes motifs from the preceding song, while introducing new ones."

Much of his life and his whole career coincided with the struggle between Athens and Sparta for hegemony in Greece but he didn't live to see the final defeat of his city.

Euripides fell out of favour with his fellow Athenian citizens and retired to the court of Archelaus, king of Macedon, who treated him with consideration and affection.

At his death, in around 406BC, he was mourned by the king, who, refusing the request of the Athenians that his remains be carried back to the Greek city, buried him with much splendor within his own dominions. His tomb was placed at the confluence of two streams, near Arethusa in Macedonia, and a cenotaph was built to his memory on the road from Athens towards the Piraeus.

Index of Contents

THE PERSONS
ANDROMACHE MAID OF ANDROMACHE
CHORUS OF PHTHIAN WOMEN
HERMIONE, daughter of MENELAUS and wife of Neoptolemus
MENELAUS, King of Sparta MOLOSSUS, son of ANDROMACHE and Neoptolemus
PELEUS, father of Achilles
NURSE OF HERMIONE ORESTES, son of Agamemnon
MESSENGER THETIS, the goddess, wife of PELEUS

SCENE

Before the temple of Thetis in Thessaly. The palace of Achilles is nearby.

ANDROMACHE

ANDROMACHE, dressed as a suppliant, is clinging to the altar in front of the temple.

ANDROMACHE
O city of Thebes, glory of Asia, whence on a day I came to Priam's princely home with many a rich and costly thing in my dower, affianced unto Hector to be the mother of his children, I Andromache, envied name in days of yore, but now of all women that have been or yet shall be the most unfortunate; for I have lived to see my husband Hector slain by Achilles, and the babe Astyanax, whom I bore my lord, hurled from the towering battlements, when the Hellenes sacked our Trojan home; and I myself am come to Hellas as a slave, though I was esteemed a daughter of a race most free, given to Neoptolemus that island-prince, and set apart for him as his special prize from the spoils of Troy. And here I dwell upon the boundaries of Phthia and Pharsalia's town, where Thetis erst, the goddess of the sea, abode with Peleus apart from the world, avoiding the throng of men; wherefore the folk of Thessaly call it the sacred place of Thetis, in honour of the goddess's marriage. Here dwells the son of Achilles and suffers Peleus still to rule Pharsalia, not wishing to assume the sceptre while the old man lives. Within these halls have borne a boy to the son of Achilles, my master. Now aforetime for all my misery I ever had a hope to lead me on, that, if my child were safe, I might find some help and protection from my woes; but since my lord in scorn of his bondmaid's charms hath wedded that Spartan Hermione, I am

tormented by her most cruelly; for she saith that I by secret enchantment am making her barren and distasteful to her husband, and that I design to take her place in this house, ousting her the rightful mistress by force; whereas I at first submitted against my will and now have resigned my place; be almighty Zeus my witness that it was not of my own free will I became her rival!

But I cannot convince her, and she longs to kill me, and her father Menelaus is an accomplice in this. E'en now is he within, arrived from Sparta for this very purpose, while I in terror am come to take up position here in the shrine of Thetis adjoining the house, if haply it may save me from death; for Peleus and his descendants hold it in honour as symbol of his marriage with the Nereid. My only son am I secretly conveying to a neighbour's house in fear for his life. For his sire stands not by my side to lend his aid and cannot avail his child at all, being absent in the land of Delphi, where he is offering recompense to Loxias for the madness he committed, when on a day he went to Pytho and demanded of Phoebus satisfaction for his father's death, if haply his prayer might avert those past sins and win for him the god's goodwill hereafter.

[The **MAID OF ANDROMACHE** enters.]

MAID
Mistress mine, be sure I do not hesitate to call thee by that name, seeing that I thought it thy right in thine own house also, when we dwelt in Troy-land; as I was ever thy friend and thy husband's while yet he was alive, so now have I come with strange tidings, in terror lest any of our masters learn hereof but still out of pity for thee; for Menelaus and his daughter are forming dire plots against thee, whereof thou must beware.

ANDROMACHE
Ah! kind companion of my bondage, for such thou art to her, who, erst thy queen, is now sunk in misery; what are they doing? What new schemes are they devising in their eagerness to take away my wretched life?

MAID
Alas! poor lady, they intend to slay thy son, whom thou hast privily conveyed from out the house.

ANDROMACHE
Ah me! Has she heard that my babe was put out of her reach? Who told her? Woe is me! how utterly undone!

MAID
I know not, but thus much of their schemes I heard myself; and Menelaus has left the house to fetch him.

ANDROMACHE
Then am I lost; ah, my child! those vultures twain will take and slay thee; while he who is called thy father lingers still in Delphi.

MAID
True, for had he been here thou wouldst not have fared so hardly, am sure; but, as it is, thou art friendless.

ANDROMACHE

Have no tidings come that Peleus may arrive?

MAID

He is too old to help thee if he came.

ANDROMACHE

And yet I sent for him more than once.

MAID

Surely thou dost not suppose that any of thy messengers heed thee?

ANDROMACHE

Why should they? Wilt thou then go for me?

MAID

How shall I explain my long absence from the house?

ANDROMACHE

Thou art a woman; thou canst invent a hundred ways.

MAID

There is a risk, for Hermione keeps no careless guard.

ANDROMACHE

Dost look to that? Thou art disowning thy friends in distress.

MAID

Not so; never taunt me with that. I will go, for of a truth a woman and a slave is not of much account, e'en if aught befall me.

[The **MAID** withdraws.]

ANDROMACHE

Go then, while I will tell to heaven the lengthy tale of lamentation, mourning, and weeping, that has ever been my hard lot; for 'tis woman's way to delight in present misfortunes even to keeping them always on her tongue and lips. But I have many reasons, not merely one for tears,—my city's fall, my Hector's death, the hardness of the lot to which I am bound, since I fell on slavery's evil days undeservedly. 'Tis never right to call a son of man happy, till thou hast seen his end, to judge from the way he passes it how he will descend to that other world.

[She begins to chant.]

'Twas no bride Paris took with him to the towers of Ilium, but curse to his bed when he brought Helen to her bower. For her sake, Troy, did eager warriors, sailing from Hellas in a thousand ships, capture and make thee a prey to fire and sword; and the son of sea-born Thetis mounted on his chariot dragged my husband Hector round the walls, ah woe is me! while I was hurried from my chamber to the beach, with slavery's hateful pall upon me. And many tear I shed as I left my city, my bridal bower, and my husband in the dust. Woe, woe is me! why should I prolong my life, to serve Hermione? Her cruelty it is that drives me hither to the image of the goddess to throw my suppliant arms about it, melting to tears as doth a spring that gushes from the rock.

[The **CHORUS OF PHTHIAN WOMEN** enters.]

CHORUS [singing, strophe 1]
Lady, thus keeping thy weary station without pause upon the floor of Thetis' shrine, Phthian though I am, to thee a daughter of Asia I come, to see if I can devise some remedy for these perplexing troubles, which have involved thee and Hermione in fell discord, because to thy sorrow thou sharest with her the love of Achilles' son.

[antistrophe 1]

Recognize thy position, weigh the present evil into the which thou art come. Thou art a Trojan captive; thy rival is thy mistress, a true-born daughter of Sparta. Leave then this home of sacrifice, the shrine of our sea-goddess. How can it avail thee to waste thy comeliness and disfigure it by weeping by reason of a mistress's harsh usage? Might will prevail against thee; why vainly toil in thy feebleness?

[strophe 2]

Come, quit the bright sanctuary of the Nereid divine. Recognize that thou art in bondage on a foreign soil, in a strange city, where thou seest none of all thy friends, luckless lady, cast on evil days.

[antistrophe 2]

Yea, I did pity thee most truly, Trojan dame, when thou camest to this house; but from fear of my mistress I hold my peace, albeit I sympathize with thee, lest she, whom Zeus's daughter bore, discover my good will toward thee.

[**HERMIONE** enters, in complete royal regalia.]

HERMIONE
With a crown of golden workmanship upon my head and about my body this embroidered robe am I come hither; no presents these I wear from the palace of Achilles or Peleus, but gifts my father Menelaus gave me together with a sumptuous dower from Sparta in Laconia, to insure me freedom of speech. Such is my answer to you; [to the **CHORUS**] but as for thee, slave and captive, thou wouldst fain oust me and secure this palace for thyself, and thanks to thy enchantment I am hated by my husband; thou it is that hast made my womb barren and cheated my hopes; for Asia's daughters have clever heads for such villainy; yet will I check thee therefrom, nor shall this temple of the Nereid avail thee aught, no! neither its altar or shrine, but thou shalt die. But if or god or man should haply wish to save thee, thou must atone for thy proud thoughts of happier days now past by humbling thyself and crouching prostrate at my knees, by sweeping out my halls, and by learning, as thou sprinklest water from a golden ewer, where thou now art. Here is no Hector, no Priam with his gold, but a city of Hellas. Yet thou, miserable woman, hast gone so far in wantonness that thou canst lay thee down with the son of the very man that slew thy husband, and bear children to the murderer. Such is all the race of barbarians; father and daughter, mother and son, sister and brother mate together; the nearest and dearest stain their path with each other's blood, and no law restrains such horrors. Bring not these

crimes amongst us, for here we count it shame that one man should have the control of two wives, and men are content to turn to one lawful love, that is, all who care to live an honourable life.

LEADER OF THE CHORUS
Women are by nature somewhat jealous, and do ever show the keenest hate to rivals in their love.

ANDROMACHE
Ah! well-a-day! Youth is a bane to mortals, in every case, that is, where a man embraces injustice in his early days. Now I am afraid that my being a slave will prevent thee listening to me in spite of many a just plea, or if I win my case, I fear I may be damaged on this very ground, for the high and mighty cannot brook refuting arguments from their inferiors; still I will not be convicted of betraying my own cause. Tell me, proud young wife, what assurance can make me confident of wresting from thee thy lawful lord? Is it that Laconia's capital yields to Phrygia? is it that my fortune outstrips thine? or that in me thou seest a free woman? Am I so elated by my youth, my full healthy figure, the extent of my city, the number of my friends that I wish to supplant thee in thy home? Is my purpose to take thy place and rear myself a race of slaves, mere appendages to my misery? or, supposing thou bear no children, will any one endure that sons of mine should rule o'er Phthia? Ah no! there is the love that Hellas bears me, both for Hector's sake and for my own humble rank forsooth, that never knew a queen's estate in Troy. 'Tis not my sorcery that makes thy husband hate thee, nay, but thy own failure to prove thyself his help-meet. Herein lies love's only charm; 'tis not beauty, lady, but virtuous acts that win our husbands' hearts. And though it gall thee to be told so, albeit thy city in Laconia is no doubt mighty fact, yet thou findest no place for his Scyros, displaying wealth 'midst poverty and setting Menelaus above Achilles: and that is what alienates thy lord. Take heed; for a woman, though bestowed upon worthless husband, must be with him content, and ne'er advance presumptuous claims. Suppose thou hadst wedded a prince of Thrace, the land of flood and melting snow, where one lord shares his affections with a host of wives, wouldst thou have slain them? If so, thou wouldst have set a stigma of insatiate lust on all our sex. A shameful charge! And yet herein we suffer more than men, though we make a good stand against it. Ah! my dear lord Hector, for thy sake would I e'en brook a rival, if ever Cypris led thee astray, and oft in days gone by I held thy bastard babes to my own breast, to spare thee any cause for grief. By this course I bound my husband to me by virtue's chains, whereas thou wilt never so much as let the drops of dew from heaven above settle on thy lord, in thy jealous fear. Oh! seek not to surpass thy mother in hankering after men, for 'tis well that all wise children should avoid the habits of such evil mothers.

LEADER
Mistress mine, be persuaded to come to terms with her, as far as readily comes within thy power.

HERMIONE
Why this haughty tone, this bandying of words, as if, forsooth, thou, not I, wert the virtuous wife?

ANDROMACHE
Thy present claims at any rate give thee small title thereto.

HERMIONE
Woman, may my bosom never harbour such ideas as thine!

ANDROMACHE
Thou art young to speak on such a theme as this.

HERMIONE

As for thee, thou dost not speak thereof, but, as thou canst, dost put it into action against me.

ANDROMACHE

Canst thou not conceal thy pangs of jealousy?

HERMIONE

What! doth not every woman put this first of all?

ANDROMACHE

Yes, if her experiences are happy; otherwise, there is no honour in speaking of them.

HERMIONE

Barbarians' laws are not a standard for our city.

ANDROMACHE

Alike in Asia and in Hellas infamy attends base actions.

HERMIONE

Clever, clever quibbler! yet die thou must and shalt.

ANDROMACHE

Dost see the image of Thetis with her eye upon thee?

HERMIONE

A bitter foe to thy country because of the death of Achilles.

ANDROMACHE

'Twas not I that slew him, but Helen that mother of thine.

HERMIONE

Pray, is it thy intention to probe my wounds yet deeper?

ANDROMACHE

Behold, I am dumb, my lips are closed.

HERMIONE

Tell me that which was my only reason for coming hither.

ANDROMACHE

No! all I tell thee is, thou hast less wisdom than thou needest.

HERMIONE

Wilt thou leave these hallowed precincts of the sea-goddess?

ANDROMACHE

Yes, if I am not to die for it; otherwise, I never will.

HERMIONE

Since that is thy resolve, I shall not even wait my lord's return.

ANDROMACHE

Nor yet will I, at any rate ere that, surrender to thee.

HERMIONE

I will bring fire to bear on thee, and pay no heed to thy entreaties.

ANDROMACHE

Kindle thy blaze then; the gods will witness it.

HERMIONE

And make thy flesh to writhe by cruel wounds.

ANDROMACHE

Begin thy butchery, stain the altar of the goddess with blood, for she will visit thy iniquity.

HERMIONE

Barbarian creature, hardened in impudence, wilt thou brave death itself? Still will I find speedy means to make these quit this seat of thy free will; such a bait have I to lure thee with. But I will hide my meaning, which the event itself shall soon declare. Yes, keep thy seat, for I will make thee rise, though molten lead is holding thee there, before Achilles' son, thy trusted champion, arrive.

[**HERMIONE** departs.]

ANDROMACHE

My trusted champion, yes! how strange it is, that though some god hath devised cures for mortals against the venom of reptiles, no man ever yet hath discovered aught to cure a woman's venom, which is far worse than viper's sting or scorching flame; so terrible a curse are we to mankind.

CHORUS [singing, strophe 1]

Ah! what sorrows did the son of Zeus and Maia herald, in the day he came to Ida's glen, guiding that fair young trio of goddesses, all girded for the fray in bitter rivalry about their beauty, to the shepherd's fold where dwelt the youthful herdsman all alone by the hearth of his lonely hut.

[antistrophe 1]

Soon as they reached the wooded glen, in gushing mountain springs they bathed their dazzling skin, then sought the son of Priam, comparing their rival charms in more than rancorous phrase. But Cypris won the day by her deceitful promises, sweet-sounding words, but fraught with ruthless overthrow to Phrygia's hapless town and Ilium's towers.

[strophe 2]

Would God his mother had smitten him a cruel death-blow on the head before he made his home on Ida's slopes, in the hour Cassandra, standing by the holy bay-tree, cried out, "Slay him, for he will bring most grievous bane on Priam's town." To every prince she went, to every elder sued for the babe's destruction.

[antistrophe 2]

Ah! had they listened, Ilium's daughters neer had felt the yoke of slavery, and thou, lady, hadst been established in the royal palace; and Hellas had been freed of all the anguish she suffered during those ten long years her sons went wandering, spear in hand, around the walls of Troy; brides had never been left desolate, nor hoary fathers childless.

[**MENELAUS** and his **RETINUE** enter. He is leading **MOLOSSUS** by the hand.]

MENELAUS
Behold I bring thy son with me, whom thou didst steal away to a neighbour's house without my daughter's knowledge. Thou wert so sure this image of the goddess would protect thee and those who hid him, but thou hast not proved clever enough for Menelaus. And so if thou refuse to leave thy station here, he shall be slain instead of thee. Wherefore weigh it well: wilt die thyself, or see him slain for the sin whereof thou art guilty against me and my daughter?

ANDROMACHE
O fame, fame! full many a man ere now of no account hast thou to high estate exalted. Those, indeed, who truly have a fair repute, I count blest; but those who get it by false pretences, I will never allow have aught but the accidental appearance of wisdom. Thou for instance, caitiff that thou art, didst thou ever wrest Troy from Priam with thy picked troops of Hellenes? thou that hast raised such a storm, at the word of thy daughter, a mere child, and hast entered the lists with a poor captive; unworthy I count thee of Troy's capture, and Troy still more disgraced by thy victory. Those who only in appearance are men of sense make an outward show, but inwardly resemble the common herd, save it be in wealth, which is their chiefest strength.

Come now, Menelaus, let us carry through this argument. Suppose I am slain by thy daughter, and she work her will on me, yet can she never escape the pollution of murder, and public opinion will make thee too an accomplice in this deed of blood, for thy share in the business must needs implicate thee. But even supposing I escape death myself, will ye kill my child? Even then, how will his father brook the murder of his child? Troy has no such coward's tale to tell of him; nay, he will follow duty's call; his actions will prove him a worthy scion of Peleus and Achilles. Thy daughter will be thrust forth from his house; and what wilt thou say when seeking to betroth her to another? wilt say her virtue made her leave a worthless lord? Nay, that will be false. Who then will wed her? wilt thou keep her without a husband in thy halls, grown grey in widowhood? Unhappy wretch! dost not see the flood-gates of trouble opening wide for thee? How many a wrong against a wife wouldst thou prefer thy daughter to have found to suffering what I now describe? We ought not on trifling grounds to promote great ills; nor should men, if we women are so deadly a curse, bring their nature down to our level. No! if, as thy daughter asserts, I am practising sorcery against her and making her barren, right willingly will I, without any crouching at altars, submit in my own person to the penalty that lies in her husband's hands, seeing that I am no less chargeable with injuring him if I make him childless. This is my case; but for thee, there is one thing I fear in thy disposition; it was a quarrel for a woman that really induced thee to destroy poor Ilium's town.

LEADER OF THE CHORUS

Thou hast said too much for a woman speaking to men; that discretion hath shot away its last shaft from thy soul's quiver.

MENELAUS

Women, these are petty matters, unworthy, as thou sayest, of my despotic sway, unworthy too of Hellas. Yet mark this well; his special fancy of the hour is of more moment to a man than Troy's capture. I then have set myself to help my daughter because I consider her loss of wife's rights most grave; for whatever else a woman suffers is second to this; if she loses her husband's love she loses her life therewith. Now, as it is right Neoptolemus should rule my slaves, so my friends and I should have control of his; for friends, if they be really friends, keep nothing to themselves, but have all in common. So if I wait for the absent instead of making the best arrangement I can at once of my affairs, I show weakness, not wisdom. Arise then, leave the goddess's shrine, for by thy death this child escapeth his, whereas, if thou refuse to die, I will slay him; for one of you twain must perish.

ANDROMACHE

Ah me! 'tis a bitter lot thou art offering about my life; whether I take it or not I am equally unfortunate. Attend to me, thou who for a trifling cause art committing an awful crime. Why art thou bent on slaying me? What reason hast thou? What city have I betrayed? Which of thy children was ever slain by me? What house have I fired? I was forced to be my master's concubine; and spite of that wilt thou slay me, not him who is to blame, passing by the cause and hurrying to the inevitable result? Ah me! my sorrows! Woe for my hapless country! How cruel my fate! Why had I to be a mother too and take upon me a double load of suffering? Yet why do I mourn the past, and o'er the present never shed a tear or compute its griefs? I that saw Hector butchered and dragged behind the chariot, and Ilium, piteous sight! one sheet of flame, while I was baled away by the hair of my head to the Argive ships in slavery, and on my arrival in Phthia was given to Hector's murderer as his mistress. What pleasure then has life for me? Whither am I to turn my gaze? to the present or the past? My babe alone was left me, the light of my life, and him these ministers of death would slay. No! they shall not, if my poor life can save him; for if he be saved, hope in him lives on, while to me 'twere shame to refuse to die for my son. Lo! here I leave the altar and give myself into your hands, to cut or stab, to bind or hang. Ah! my child, to Hades now thy mother passes to save thy dear life. Yet if thou escape thy doom, remember me, my sufferings and my death, and tell thy father how I fared, with fond caress and streaming eye and arms thrown round his neck. Ah! yes, his children are to every man as his own soul; and whoso sneers at this through inexperience, though he suffers less anguish, yet tastes the bitter in his cup of bliss.

LEADER

Thy tale with pity fills me; for every man alike, stranger though he be, feels pity for another's distress. Menelaus, 'tis thy duty to reconcile thy daughter and this captive, giving her a respite from sorrow.

MENELAUS

Ho! sirrahs, seize this woman—

[His **ATTENDANTS** swiftly carry out the order.]

Hold her fast; for 'tis no welcome story she will have to hear. It was to make thee leave the holy altar of the goddess that I held thy child's death before thy eyes, and so induced thee to give thyself up to me to die. So stands thy case, be well assured; but as for this child, my daughter shall decide whether she will slay him or no. Get thee hence into the house, and there learn to bridle thy insolence in speaking to the free, slave that thou art.

ANDROMACHE

Alas! thou hast by treachery beguiled me; I was deceived.

MENELAUS

Proclaim it to the world; I do not deny it.

ANDROMACHE

Is this counted cleverness amongst you who dwell by the Eurotas?

MENELAUS

Yes, and amongst Trojans too, that those who suffer should retaliate.

ANDROMACHE

Thinkest thou God's hand is shortened, and that thou wilt not be punished?

MENELAUS

Whene'er that comes, I am ready to bear it. But thy life will I have.

ANDROMACHE

Wilt likewise slay this tender chick, whom thou hast snatched from 'neath my wing?

MENELAUS

Not I, but I will give him to my daughter to slay if she will.

ANDROMACHE

Ah me! why not begin my mourning then for thee, my child?

MENELAUS

Of a truth 'tis no very sure hope that he has left.

ANDROMACHE

O citizens of Sparta, the bane of all the race of men, schemers of guile, and masters in lying, devisers of evil plots, with crooked minds and tortuous methods and ne'er one honest thought, 'tis wrong that ye should thrive in Hellas. What crime is wanting in your list? How rife is murder with you! How covetous ye are! One word upon your lips, another in your heart, this is what men always find with you. Perdition catch ye! Still death is not so grievous, as thou thinkest, to me. No! for my life ended in the day that hapless Troy was destroyed with my lord, that glorious warrior, whose spear oft made a coward like thee quit the field and seek thy ship. But now against a woman hast thou displayed the terrors of thy panoply, my would-be murderer. Strike then! for this my tongue shall never flatter thee or that daughter of thine. For though thou wert of great account in Sparta, why so was I in Troy. And if I am now in sorry plight, presume not thou on this; thou too mayst be so yet.

[**MENELAUS** and his guards lead **ANDROMACHE** out.]

CHORUS [singing, strophe 1]

Never, oh! never will I commend rival wives or sons of different mothers, a cause of strife, of bitterness, and grief in every house. would have a husband content with one wife whose rights he shareth with no other.

[antistrophe 1]

Not even in states is dual monarchy better to bear than undivided rule; it only doubles burdens and causes faction amongst the citizens. Often too will the Muse sow strife 'twixt rivals in the art of minstrelsy.

[strophe 2]

Again, when strong winds are drifting mariners, the divided counsel of the wise does not best avail for steering, and their collective wisdom has less weight than the inferior mind of the single man who has sole authority; for this is the essence of power alike in house and state, whene'er men care to find the proper moment.

[antistrophe 2]

This Spartan, the daughter of the great chief Menelaus, proves this; for she hath kindled hot fury against a rival, and is bent on slaying the hapless Trojan maid and her child to further her bitter quarrel. 'Tis a murder gods and laws and kindness all forbid. Ah! lady, retribution for this deed will yet visit thee.

But lo! before the house I see those two united souls, condemned to die. Alas! for thee, poor lady, and for thee, unhappy child, who art dying on account of thy mother's marriage, though thou hast no share therein and canst not be blamed by the royal house.

[**ANDROMACHE** enters, her arms bound. Her son clings to her. **MENELAUS** and the **GUARDS** follow, intent on accomplishing the murder. The following lines are chanted responsively.]

ANDROMACHE
Behold me journeying on the downward path, my hands so tightly bound with cords that they bleed.

MOLOSSUS
O mother, mother mine! I too share thy downward path, nestling 'neath thy wing.

ANDROMACHE
A cruel sacrifice! ye rulers of Phthia!

MOLOSSUS
Come, father! succour those thou lovest.

ANDROMACHE
Rest there, my babe, my darling! on thy mother's bosom, e'en in death and in the grave.

MOLOSSUS
Ah, woe is me! what will become of me and thee too, mother mine?

MENELAUS
Away, to the world below! from hostile towers ye came, the pair of you; two different causes necessitate your deaths; my sentence takes away thy life, and my daughter Hermione's requires his; for it would be the height of folly to leave our foemen's sons, when we might kill them and remove the danger from our house.

ANDROMACHE
O husband mine! I would I had thy strong arm and spear to aid me, son of Priam.

MOLOSSUS
Ah, woe is me! what spell can I now find to turn death's stroke aside?

ANDROMACHE
Embrace thy master's knees, my child, and pray to him.

MOLOSSUS
Spare, O spare my life, kind master!

ANDROMACHE
Mine eyes are wet with tears, which trickle down my cheeks, as doth a sunless spring from a smooth rock. Ah me!

MOLOSSUS
What remedy, alas! can I provide me 'gainst my ills?

MENELAUS
Why fall at my knees in supplication? hard as the rock and deaf as the wave am I. My own friends have I helped, but for thee have no tie of affection; for verily it cost me a great part of my life to capture Troy and thy mother; so thou shalt reap the fruit thereof and into Hades' halls descend.

LEADER OF THE CHORUS
Behold! I see Peleus drawing nigh; with aged step he hasteth hither.

[**PELEUS** enters with an **ATTENDANT**.]

PELEUS [calling out as he comes in sight]
What means this? I ask you and your executioner; why is the palace in an uproar? give a reason; what mean your lawless machinations? Menelaus, hold thy hand. Seek not to outrun justice. [To his **ATTENDANT**] Forward! faster, faster! for this matter, methinks, admits of no delay; now if ever would I fain resume the vigour of my youth. First however will breathe new life into this captive, being to her as the breeze that blows a ship before the wind. Tell me, by what right have they pinioned thine arms and are dragging thee and thy child away? Like a ewe with her lamb art thou led to the slaughter, while I and thy lord were far away.

ANDROMACHE
Behold them that are haling me and my child to death, e'en as thou seest, aged prince. Why should I tell thee? For not by one urgent summons alone but by countless messengers have I sent for thee. No doubt thou knowest by hearsay of the strife in this house with this man's daughter, and the reason of my ruin.

So now they have torn and are dragging me from the altar of Thetis, the goddess of thy chiefest adoration and the mother of thy gallant son, without any proper trial, yea, and without waiting for my absent master; because, forsooth, they knew my defencelessness and my child's, whom they mean to slay with me his hapless mother, though he has done no harm. But to thee, O sire, I make my supplication, prostrate at thy knees, though my hand cannot touch thy friendly beard; save me, I adjure thee, reverend sir, or to thy shame and my sorrow shall we be slain.

PELEUS

Loose her bonds, I say, ere some one rue it; untie her folded hands.

MENELAUS

I forbid it, for besides being a match for thee, I have a far better right to her.

PELEUS

What! art thou come hither to set my house in order? Art not content with ruling thy Spartans?

MENELAUS

She is my captive; I took her from Troy.

PELEUS

Aye, but my son's son received her as his prize.

MENELAUS

Is not all I have his, and all his mine?

PELEUS

For good, but not evil ends; and surely not for murderous violence.

MENELAUS

Never shalt thou wrest her from my grasp.

PELEUS

With this good staff I'll stain thy head with blood!

MENELAUS

Just touch me and see! Approach one step!

PELEUS

What! shalt thou rank with men? chief of cowards, son of cowards! What right hast thou to any place 'mongst men? Thou who didst let Phrygian rob thee of thy wife, leaving thy home without bolt or guard, as if forsooth the cursed woman thou hadst there was a model of virtue. No! a Spartan maid could not be chaste, e'en if she would, who leaves her home and bares her limbs and lets her robe float free, to share with youths their races and their sports,—customs I cannot away with. Is it any wonder then that ye fail to educate your women in virtue? Helen might have asked thee this, seeing that she said goodbye to thy affection and tripped off with her young gallant to a foreign land. And yet for her sake thou didst marshal all the hosts of Hellas and lead them to Ilium, whereas thou shouldst have shown thy loathing for her by refusing to stir a spear, once thou hadst found her false; yea, thou shouldst have let her stay there, and even paid a price to save ever having her back again. But that was not at all the way thy thoughts were turned; wherefore many a brave life hast thou ended, and many an aged mother hast thou left childless in her home, and grey-haired sires of gallant sons hast reft. Of that sad band am I member, seeing in thee Achilles' murderer like a malignant fiend; for thou and thou alone hast returned from Troy without a scratch, bringing back thy splendid weapons in their splendid cases just as they went. As for me, I ever told that amorous boy to form no alliance with thee nor take unto his home an evil mother's child; for daughters bear the marks of their mothers' ill-repute into their new homes. Wherefore, ye wooers, take heed to this my warning: "Choose the daughter of a good mother." And more than this, with what wanton insult didst thou treat thy brother, bidding him sacrifice his daughter in his simpleness! So fearful wast thou of losing thy worthless wife. Then after capturing Troy,—for thither too will I accompany thee,—thou didst not slay that woman, when she was in thy power; but as soon as thine eyes caught sight of her breast, thy sword was dropped and thou didst take her kisses, fondling the shameless traitress, too weak to stem thy hot desire, thou caitiff wretch! Yet spite of all thou art the man to come and work havoc in my grandson's halls when he is absent, seeking to slay with all indignity a poor weak woman and her babe: but that babe shall one day make thee and thy daughter in thy home rue it, e'en though his birth be trebly base. Yea, for oft ere now hath seed, sown on barren soil, prevailed o'er rich deep tilth, and many bastard has proved a better man than children better born. Take thy daughter hence with thee! Far better is it for mortals to have a poor honest man either as married kin or friend than a wealthy knave; but as for thee, thou art a thing of naught.

LEADER
The tongue from trifling causes contrives to breed great strife 'mongst men; wherefore are the wise most careful not to bring about a quarrel with their friends.

MENELAUS
Why, pray, should one call these old men wise, or those who once had a reputation in Hellas for being so? when thou, the great Peleus, son of famous father, kin to me through marriage, employest language disgraceful to thyself and abusive of me because of a barbarian woman, though thou shouldst have banished her far beyond the streams of Nile or Phasis, and ever encouraged me; seeing that she comes from Asia's continent where fell so many of the sons of Hellas, victims to the spear; and likewise because she shared in the spilling of thy son's blood; for Paris who slew thy son Achilles, was brother to Hector, whose wife she was. And dost thou enter the same abode with her, and deign to let her share thy board, and suffer her to rear her brood of vipers in thy house? But I, after all this foresight for thee, old man, and myself, am to have her torn from my clutches for wishing to slay her. Yet come now, for 'tis no disgrace to argue; suppose my daughter has no child, while this woman's sons grow up, wilt thou set them up to rule the land of Phthia, barbarians born and bred to lord it over Hellenes? Am I then so void of sense because I hate injustice, and thou so full of cleverness? Consider yet another point; say thou hadst given a daughter of thine to some citizen, and hadst then seen her thus treated, wouldst thou have sat looking on in silence? I trow not. Dost thou then for a foreigner rail thus at thy nearest friends? Again, thou mayst say, husband and wife have an equally strong case if she is wronged by him, and similarly if he find her guilty of indiscretion in his house; yet while he has ample powers in his own hands, she depends on parents and friends for her case. Surely then I am right in helping my own kin! Thou art in thy dotage; for thou wilt do me more good by speaking of my generalship than by concealing it. Helen's trouble was not of her own choosing, but sent by heaven, and it proved a great benefit to Hellas; her sons, till then untried in war or arms, turned to deeds of prowess, and it is experience which teaches man all he knows. I showed my wisdom in refraining from slaying my wife, directly I caught sight of her. Would that thou too hadst ne'er slain Phocus! All this I bring before thee in pure good-will, not from anger. But if thou resent it, thy tongue may wag till it ache, yet shall I gain by prudent forethought.

LEADER
Cease now from idle words, 'twere better far, for fear ye both alike go wrong.

PELEUS
Alas! what evil customs now prevail in Hellas! Whene'er the host sets up a trophy o'er the foe, men no more consider this the work of those who really toiled, but the general gets the credit for it. Now he was but one among ten thousand others to brandish his spear; he only did the work of one; but yet he wins more praise than they. Again, as magistrates in all the grandeur of office they scorn the common folk, though they are naught themselves; whereas those others are ten thousand times more wise than they, if daring combine with judgment. Even so thou and thy brother, exalted by the toilsome efforts of others, now take your seats in all the swollen pride of Trojan fame and Trojan generalship. But I will teach thee henceforth to consider Idaean Paris a foe less terrible than Peleus, unless forthwith thou pack from this roof, thou and thy childless daughter too, whom my own true son will hale through his halls by the hair of her head; for her barrenness will not let her endure fruitfulness in others, because she has no children herself. Still if misfortune prevents her bearing offspring, is that a reason why we should be left childless? Begone! ye varlets, let her go! I will soon see if anyone will hinder me from loosing her hands. [to **ANDROMACHE**] Arise; these trembling hands of mine will untie the twisted thongs that bind thee. Out on thee, coward! is this how thou hast galled her wrists? Didst think thou wert lashing up a lion or bull? or wert afraid she would snatch a sword and defend herself against thee? Come, child, nestle to thy mother's arms; help me loose her bonds; I will yet rear thee in Phthia to be their bitter foe. If your reputation for prowess and the battles ye have fought were taken from you Spartans, in all else, be very sure, you have not your inferiors.

LEADER
The race of old men practises no restraint; and their testiness makes it hard to check them.

MENELAUS
Thou art only too ready to rush into abuse; while, as for me, I came to Phthia by constraint and have therefore no intention either of doing or suffering anything mean. Now must I return home, for I have no time to waste; for there is a city not so very far from Sparta, which aforetime was friendly but now is hostile; against her will I march with my army and bring her into subjection. And when I have arranged that matter as I wish, I will return; and face to face with my son-in-law I will give my version of the story and hear his. And if he punish her, and for the future she exercise self-control, she shall find me do the like; but if he storm, I'll storm as well; and every act of mine shall be a reflex of his own. As for thy babbling, I can bear it easily; for, like to a shadow as thou art, thy voice is all thou hast, and thou art powerless to do aught but talk.

[**MENELAUS** and his retinue withdraw.]

PELEUS
Lead on, my child, safe beneath my sheltering wing, and thou too, poor lady; for thou art come into a quiet haven after the rude storm.

ANDROMACHE
Heaven reward thee and all thy race, old sire, for having saved my child and me his hapless mother! Only beware lest they fall upon us twain in some lonely spot upon the road and force me from thee, when they see thy age, my weakness, and this child's tender years; take heed to this, that we be not a second time made captive, after escaping now.

PELEUS
Forbear such words, prompted by a woman's cowardice. Go on thy way; who will lay a finger on you? Methinks he will do it to his cost, For by heaven's grace I rule o'er many a knight and spearman bold in my kingdom of Phthia; yea, and myself can still stand straight, no bent old man as thou dost think; such a fellow as that a mere look from me will put to flight in spite of my years. For e'en an old man, be he brave, is worth a host of raw youths; for what avails a fine figure if a man is coward?

[**PELEUS**, **ANDROMACHE**, and **MOLOSSUS** go out.]

CHORUS [singing, strophe]
Oh! to have never been born, or sprung from noble sires, the heir to mansions richly stored; for if aught untoward e'er befall, there is no lack of champions for sons of noble parents, and there is honour and glory for them when they are proclaimed scions of illustrious lines; time detracts not from the legacy these good men leave, but the light of their goodness still burns on when they are dead.

[antistrophe]

Better is it not to win a discreditable victory, than to make justice miscarry by an invidious exercise of power; for such a victory, though men think it sweet for the moment, grows barren in time and comes near being a stain on a house. This is the life I commend, this the life I set before me as my ideal, to exercise no authority beyond what is right either in the marriage-chamber or in the state.

[epode]

O aged son of Aeacus! now am I sure that thou wert with the Lapithae, wielding thy famous spear, when they fought the Centaurs; and on Argo's deck didst pass the cheerless strait beyond the sea-beat Symplegades on her voyage famed; and when in days long gone the son of Zeus spread slaughter round Troy's famous town, thou too didst share his triumphant return to Europe.

[The **NURSE OF HERMIONE** enters.]

NURSE
Alas! good friends, what a succession of troubles is to-day provided us! My mistress Hermione within the house, deserted by her father and in remorse for her monstrous deed in plotting the death of Andromache and her child, is bent on dying; for she is afraid her husband will in requital for this expel her with dishonour from his house or put her to death, because she tried to slay the innocent. And the servants that watch her can scarce restrain her efforts to hang herself, scarce catch the sword and wrest it from her hand. So bitter is her anguish, and she hath recognized the villainy of her former deeds. As for me, friends, I am weary of keeping my mistress from the fatal noose; do ye go in and try to save her life; for if strangers come, they prove more persuasive than the friends of every day.

LEADER OF THE CHORUS
Ah yes! I hear an outcry in the house amongst the servants, confirming the news thou hast brought. Poor sufferer! she seems about to show lively grief for her grave crimes; for she has escaped her servants' hands and is rushing from the house, eager to end her life.

[**HERMIONE** enters, in agitation. She is carrying a sword which the **NURSE** wrests from her.]

HERMIONE [chanting]
Woe, woe is me! I will rend my hair and tear cruel furrows in my cheeks.

NURSE
My child, what wilt thou do? Wilt thou disfigure thyself?

HERMIONE [chanting]
Ah me! ah me! Begone, thou fine-spun veil! float from my head away!

NURSE
Daughter, cover up thy bosom, fasten thy robe.

HERMIONE [chanting]
Why should I cover it? My crimes against my lord are manifest and clear, they cannot be hidden.

NURSE
Art so grieved at having devised thy rival's death?

HERMIONE
[chanting] Yea, I deeply mourn my fatal deeds of daring; alas! I am now accursed in all men's eyes!

NURSE
Thy husband will pardon thee this error.

HERMIONE [chanting]
Oh! why didst thou hunt me to snatch away my sword? Give, oh! give it back, dear nurse, that I may thrust it through my heart Why dost thou prevent me hanging myself?

NURSE
What! was I to let thy madness lead thee on to death?

HERMIONE [chanting]
Ah me, my destiny! Where can I find some friendly fire? To what rocky height can I climb above the sea or 'mid some wooded mountain glen, there to die and trouble but the dead?

NURSE
Why vex thyself thus? on all of us sooner or later heaven's visitation comes.

HERMIONE [chanting]
Thou hast left me, O my father, left me like a stranded bark, all alone, without an oar. My lord will surely slay me; no home is mine henceforth beneath my husband's roof. What god is there to whose statue I can as a suppliant haste? or shall I throw myself in slavish wise at slavish knees? Would I could speed away from Phthia's land on bird's dark pinion, or like that pine-built ship, the first that ever sailed betwixt the rocks Cyanean!

NURSE

My child, I can as little praise thy previous sinful excesses, committed against the Trojan captive, as thy present exaggerated terror. Thy husband will never listen to a barbarian's weak pleading and reject his marriage with thee for this. For thou wast no captive from Troy whom he wedded, but the daughter of a gallant sire, with a rich dower, from a city too of no mean prosperity. Nor will thy father forsake thee, as thou dreadest, and allow thee to be cast out from this house. Nay, enter now, nor show thyself before the palace, lest the sight of thee there bring reproach upon thee, my daughter.

[The **NURSE** departs as **ORESTES** and his attendants enter.]

LEADER
Lo! a stranger of foreign appearance from some other land comes hurrying towards us.

ORESTES
Women of this foreign land! is this the home, the palace of Achilles' son?

LEADER
Thou hast it; but who art thou to ask such a question?

ORESTES
The son of Agamemnon and Clytemnestra, by name Orestes, on ply way to the oracle of Zeus at Dodona. But now that I am come to Phthia, I am resolved to inquire about my kinswoman, Hermione of Sparta; is she alive and well? for though she dwells in a land far from my own, I love her none the less.

HERMIONE
Son of Agamemnon, thy appearing is as a haven from the storm to sailors; by thy knees I pray, have pity on me in my distress, on me of whose fortunes thou art inquiring. About thy knees I twine my arms with all the force of sacred fillets.

ORESTES
Ha! what is this? Am I mistaken or do I really see before me the queen of this palace, the daughter of Menelaus?

HERMIONE
The same, that only child whom Helen, daughter of Tyndareus, bore my father in his halls; never doubt that.

ORESTES
O saviour Phoebus, grant us respite from our woe! But what is the matter? art thou afflicted by gods or men?

HERMIONE
Partly by myself, partly by the man who wedded me, and partly by some god. On every side I see ruin.

ORESTES
Why, what misfortune could happen to a woman as yet childless, unless her honour is concerned?

HERMIONE
My very ill! Thou hast hit my case exactly.

ORESTES

On whom has thy husband set his affections in thy stead?

HERMIONE

On his captive, Hector's wife.

ORESTES

An evil case indeed, for a man to have two wives!

HERMIONE

'Tis even thus. So I resented it.

ORESTES

Didst thou with woman's craft devise a plot against thy rival?

HERMIONE

Yes, to slay her and her bastard child.

ORESTES

And didst thou slay them, or did something happen to rescue them from thee?

HERMIONE

It was old Peleus, who showed regard to the weaker side.

ORESTES

Hadst thou any accomplice in this attempted murder?

HERMIONE

My father came from Sparta for this very purpose.

ORESTES

And was he after all defeated by that old man's prowess?

HERMIONE

Oh no! but by shame; and he hath gone and left me all alone.

ORESTES

I understand; thou art afraid of thy husband for what thou hast done.

HERMIONE

Thou hast guessed it; for he will have a right to slay me. What can say for myself? Yet I beseech thee by Zeus the god of our family, send me to a land as far as possible from this, or to my father's house; for these very walls seem to cry out "Begone!" and all the land of Phthia hates me. But if my lord return ere that from the oracle of Phoebus, he will put me to death on a shameful charge, or enslave me to his mistress, whom ruled before. Maybe some one will say, "How was it thou didst go thus astray?" I was ruined by evil women who came to me and puffed me up with words like these: "Wait! wilt thou suffer that vile captive, a mere bondmaid, to dwell within thy house and share thy wedded rights? By Heaven's queen! if it were my house she should not live to reap my marriage-harvest!" And I listened to the words of these Sirens, the cunning, knavish, subtle praters, and was filled with silly thoughts. What need had I to care about my lord? I had all I wanted, wealth in plenty, a house in which I was mistress, and as for children, mine would be born in wedlock, while hers would be bastards, half-slaves to mine. Oh! never, never,—this truth will I repeat,-should men of sense, who have wives, allow women-folk to visit them in their homes, for they teach them evil; one, to gain some private end, helps to corrupt their honour; another, having made a slip herself, wants a companion in misfortune, while many are wantons; and hence it is men's houses are tainted. Wherefore keep strict guard upon the portals of your houses with bolts and bars; for these visits of strange women lead to no good result, but a world of ill.

LEADER
Thou hast given thy tongue too free a rein regarding thy own sex. I can pardon thee in this case, but still women ought to smooth over their sisters' weaknesses.

ORESTES
'Twas sage counsel he gave who taught men to hear the arguments on both sides. I, for instance, though aware of the confusion in this house, the quarrel between thee and Hector's wife, waited awhile and watched to see whether thou wouldst stay here or from fear of that captive art minded to quit these halls. Now it was not so much regard for thy message that brought me thither, as the intention of carrying thee away from this house, if, as now, thou shouldst grant me a chance of saying so. For thou wert mine formerly, but art now living with thy present husband through thy father's baseness; since he, before invading Troy's domains, betrothed thee to me, and then afterwards promised thee to thy present lord, provided he captured the city of Troy.

So, as soon as Achilles' son returned hither, I forgave thy father, but entreated the bridegroom to forego his marriage with thee, telling him all I had endured and my present misfortune; I might get a wife, I said, from amongst friends, but outside their circle 'twas no easy task for one exiled like myself from home. Thereat he grew abusive, taunting me with my mother's murder and those blood-boltered fiends. And I was humbled by the fortunes of my house, and though 'tis true, I grieved, yet did I bear my sorrow, and reluctantly departed, robbed of thy promised hand. Now therefore, since thou findest thy fortune so abruptly changed and art fallen thus on evil days and hast no help, I will take thee hence and place thee in thy father's hands. For kinship hath strong claims, and in adversity there is naught better than a kinsman's kindly aid.

HERMIONE
As for my marriage, my father must look to it; 'tis not for me to decide. Yes, take me hence as soon as may be, lest my husband come back to his house before I am gone, or Peleus hear that I am deserting his son's abode and pursue me with his swift steeds.

ORESTES
Rest easy about the old man's power; and, as for Achilles' son with all his insolence to me, never fear him; such a crafty net this hand hath woven and set for his death with knots that none can loose; whereof I will not speak before the time, but, when my plot begins to work, Delphi's rock will witness it. If but my allies in the Pythian land abide by their oaths, this same murderer of his mother will show that no one else shall marry thee my rightful bride. To his cost will he demand satisfaction of King Phoebus for his father's blood; nor shall his repentance avail him though he is now submitting to the god. No! he shall perish miserably by Apollo's hand and my false accusations; so shall he find out my enmity. For the deity upsets the fortune of them that hate him, and suffers them not to be high-minded.

[**ORESTES** and **HERMIONE** depart.]

CHORUS [singing, strophe 1]
O Phoebus! who didst fence the hill of Ilium with a fair coronal of towers, and thou, ocean-god! coursing o'er the main with thy dark steeds, wherefore did ye hand over in dishonour your own handiwork to the war-god, master of the spear, abandoning Troy to wretchedness?

[antistrophe 1]

Many a well-horsed car ye yoked on the banks of Simois, and many a bloody tournament did ye ordain with never a prize to win; and Ilium's princes are dead and gone; no longer in Troy is seen the blaze of fire on altars of the gods with the smoke of incense.

[strophe 2]

The son of Atreus is no more, slain by the hand of his wife, and she herself hath paid the debt of blood by death, and from her children's hands received her doom. The god's own bidding from his oracle was levelled against her, in the day that Agamemnon's son set forth from Argos and visited his shrine; so he slew her, aye, spilt his own mother's blood. O Phoebus, O thou power divine, how can I believe the story?

[antistrophe 2]

Anon wherever Hellenes gather, was heard the voice of lamentation, mothers weeping o'er their children's fate, as they left their homes to mate with strangers. Ah! thou art not the only one, nor thy dear ones either, on whom the cloud of grief hath fallen. Hellas had to bear the visitation, and thence the scourge crossed to Phrygia's fruitful fields, raining the bloody drops the death-god loves.

[**PELEUS** enters in haste.]

PELEUS
Ye dames of Phthia, answer my questions. I heard a vague rumour that the daughter of Menelaus had left these halls and fled; so now I am come in hot haste to learn if this be true; for it is the duty of those who are at home to labour in the interests of their absent friends.

LEADER OF THE CHORUS
Thou hast heard aright, O Peleus; ill would it become me to hide the evil case in which I now find myself; our queen has fled and left these halls.

PELEUS
What did she fear? explain that to me.

LEADER
She was afraid her lord would cast her out.

PELEUS
In return for plotting his child's death? surely not?

LEADER
Yea, and she was afraid of yon captive.

PELEUS
With whom did she leave the house? with her father?

LEADER
The son of Agamemnon came and took her hence.

PELEUS
What view hath he to further thereby? Will he marry her?

LEADER
Yes, and he is plotting thy grandson's death.

PELEUS
From an ambuscade, or meeting him fairly face to face?

LEADER
In the holy place of Loxias, leagued with Delphians.

PELEUS
God help us. This is a present danger. Hasten one of you with all speed to the Pythian altar and tell our friends there what has happened here, ere Achilles' son be slain by his enemies.

[A **MESSENGER** enters.]

MESSENGER
Woe worth the day! what evil tidings have I brought for thee, old sire, and for all who love my master! woe is me!

PELEUS
Alas! my prophetic soul hath a presentiment.

MESSENGER
Aged Peleus, hearken! Thy grandson is no more; so grievously is he smitten by the men of Delphi and the stranger from Mycenae.

LEADER
Ah! what wilt thou do, old man? Fall not; uplift thyself.

PELEUS
I am a thing of naught; death is come upon me. My voice is choked, my limbs droop beneath me.

MESSENGER
Hearken; if thou art eager also to avenge thy friends, lift up thyself and hear what happened.

PELEUS

Ah, destiny! how tightly hast thou caught me in thy toils, a poor old man at life's extremest verge! But tell me how he was taken from me, my one son's only child; unwelcome as such news is, I fain would hear it.

MESSENGER

As soon as we reached the famous soil of Phoebus, for three whole days were we feasting our eyes with the sight. And this, it seems, caused suspicion; for the folk, who dwell near the god's shrine, began to collect in groups, while Agamemnon's son, going to and fro through the town, would whisper in each man's ear malignant hints: "Do ye see yon fellow, going in and out of the god's treasure-chambers, which are full of the gold stored there by all mankind? He is come hither a second time on the same mission as before, eager to sack the temple of Phoebus." Thereon there ran an angry murmur through the city, and the magistrates flocked to their council-chamber, while those, who have charge of the god's treasures, had a guard privately placed amongst the colonnades. But we, knowing naught as yet of this, took sheep fed in the pastures of Parnassus, and went our way and stationed ourselves at the altars with vouchers and Pythian seers. And one said: "What prayer, young warrior, wouldst thou have us offer to the god? Wherefore art thou come?" And he answered: "I wish to make atonement to Phoebus for my past transgression; for once I claimed from him satisfaction for my father's blood." Thereupon the rumour, spread by Orestes, proved to have great weight, suggesting that my master was lying and had come on a shameful errand. But he crosses the threshold of the temple to pray to Phoebus before his oracle, and was busy with his burnt-offering; when a body of men armed with swords set themselves in ambush against him in the cover of the bay-trees, and Clytemnestra's son, that had contrived the whole plot was one of them. There stood the young man praying to the god in sight of all, when lo! with their sharp swords they stabbed Achilles' unprotected son from behind. But he stepped back, for it was not a mortal wound he had received, and drew his sword, and snatching armour from the pegs where it hung on a pillar, took his stand upon the altar-steps, the picture of a warrior grim; then cried he to the sons of Delphi, and asked them: "Why seek to slay me when I am come on a holy mission? What cause is there why I should die?" But of all that throng of bystanders, no man answered him a word, but they set to hurling stones. Then he, though bruised and battered by the showers of missiles from all sides, covered himself behind his mail and tried to ward off the attack, holding his shield first here, then there, at arm's length, but all of no avail; for a storm of darts, arrows and javelins, hurtling spits with double points, and butchers' knives for slaying steers, came flying at his feet; and terrible was the war-dance thou hadst then seen thy grandson dance to avoid their marksmanship. At last, when they were hemming him in on all sides, allowing him no breathing space, he left the shelter of the altar, the hearth where victims are placed, and with one bound was on them as on the Trojans of yore; and they turned and fled like doves when they see the hawk. Many fell in the confusion: some wounded, and others trodden down by one another along the narrow passages; and in that hushed holy house uprose unholy din and echoed back from the rocks. Calm and still my master stood there in his gleaming harness like a flash of light, till from the inmost shrine there came a voice of thrilling horror, stirring the crowd to make a stand. Then fell Achilles' son, smitten through the flank by some Delphian's biting blade, some fellow that slew him with a host to help; and as he fell, there was not one that did not stab him, or cast a rock and batter his corpse. So his whole body, once so fair, was marred with savage wounds. At last they cast the lifeless clay, lying near the altar, forth from the fragrant fane. And we gathered up his remains forthwith and are bringing them to thee, old prince, to mourn and weep and honour with a deep-dug tomb.

This is how that prince who vouchsafeth oracles to others, that judge of what is right for all the world, hath revenged himself on Achilles' son, remembering his ancient quarrel as a wicked man would. How then can he be wise?

[The **MESSENGER** withdraws as the body of **NEOPTOLEMUS** is carried in on a bier. The following lines between **PELEUS** and the **CHORUS** are chanted responsively.]

CHORUS
Lo! e'en now our prince is being carried on a bier from Delphi's land unto his home. Woe for him and his sad fate, and woe for thee, old sire! for this is not the welcome thou wouldst give Achilles' son, the lion's whelp; thyself too by this sad mischance dost share his evil lot.

PELEUS
Ah! woe is me! here is a sad sight for me to see and take unto my halls! Ah me! ah me! I am undone, thou city of Thessaly! My line now ends; I have no children left me in my home. Oh! the sorrows seem born to endure! What friend can I look to for relief? Ah, dear lips, and cheeks, and hands! Would thy destiny had slain the 'neath Ilium's walls beside the banks of Simois!

CHORUS
Had he so died, my aged lord, he had won him honour thereby, and thine had been the happier lot.

PELEUS
O marriage, marriage, woe to thee! thou bane of my home, thou destroyer of my city! Ah my child, my boy, would that the honour of wedding thee, fraught with evil as it was to my children and house, had not thrown o'er thee, my son, Hermione's deadly net! that the thunderbolt had slain her sooner! and that thou, rash mortal, hadst never charged the great god Phoebus with aiming that murderous shaft that spilt thy hero-father's blood!

CHORUS
Woe! woe! alas! With due observance of funeral rites will I begin the mourning for my dead master.

PELEUS
Alack and well-a-day! I take up the tearful dirge, ah me! old and wretched as I am.

CHORUS
'Tis Heaven's decree; God willed this heavy stroke.

PELEUS
O darling child, thou hast left me all alone in my halls, old and childless by thy loss.

CHORUS
Thou shouldst have died, old sire, before thy children.

PELEUS
Shall I not tear my hair, and smite upon my head with grievous blows? O city! of both my children hath Phoebus robbed me.

CHORUS
What evils thou hast suffered, what sorrows thou hast seen, thou poor old man! what shall be thy life hereafter?

PELEUS

Childless, desolate, with no limit to my grief, I must drain the cup of woe, until I die.

CHORUS

'Twas all in vain the gods wished thee joy on thy wedding day.

PELEUS

All my hopes have flown away, fallen short of my high boasts.

CHORUS

A lonely dweller in a lonely home art thou.

PELEUS

I have no city any longer; there! on the ground my sceptre do cast; and thou, daughter of Nereus, 'neath thy dim grotto, shalt see me grovelling in the dust, a ruined king.

CHORUS

Look, look!

[A dim form of divine appearance is seen hovering mid air.]

What is that moving? what influence divine am I conscious of? Look, maidens, mark it well; see, yonder is some deity, wafted through the lustrous air and alighting on the plains of Phthia, home of steeds.

THETIS [from above]

O Peleus! because of my wedded days with thee now long agone, I Thetis am come from the halls of Nereus. And first I counsel thee not to grieve to excess in thy present distress, for I too who need ne'er have borne children to my sorrow, have lost the child of our love, Achilles swift of foot, foremost of the sons of Hellas. Next will I declare why I am come, and do thou give ear. Carry yonder corpse, Achilles' son, to the Pythian altar and there bury it, a reproach to Delphi, that his tomb may proclaim the violent death he met at the hand of Orestes. And for his captive wife Andromache,—she must dwell in the Molossian land, united in honourable wedlock with Helenus, and with her this babe, the sole survivor as he is of all the line of Aeacus, for from him a succession of prosperous kings of Molossia is to go on unbroken; for the race that springs from thee and me, my aged lord, must not thus be brought to naught; no! nor Troy's line either; for her fate too is cared for by the gods, albeit her fall was due to the eager wish of Pallas. Thee too, that thou mayst know the saving grace of wedding me, will I, a goddess born and daughter of a god, release from all the ills that flesh is heir to and make a deity to know not death nor decay. From henceforth in the halls of Nereus shalt thou dwell with me, god and goddess together; thence shalt thou rise dry-shod from out the main and see Achilles, our dear son, settled in his island-home by the strand of Leuce, that is girdled by the Euxine sea. But get thee to Delphi's god-built town, carrying this corpse with thee, and, after thou hast buried him, return and settle in the cave which time hath hollowed in the Sepian rock and there abide, till from the sea I come with choir of fifty Nereids to be thy escort thence; for fate's decree thou must fulfil; such is the pleasure of Zeus. Cease then to mourn the dead; this is the lot which heaven assigns to all, and all must pay their debt to death.

PELEUS

Great queen, my honoured wife, from Nereus sprung, all hail! thou art acting herein as befits thyself and thy children. So I will stay my grief at thy bidding, goddess, and, when I have buried the dead, will seek the glens of Pelion, even the place where I took thy beauteous form to my embrace. Surely after this every prudent man will seek to marry a wife of noble stock and give his daughter to a husband good and true, never setting his heart on a worthless woman, not even though she bring a sumptuous dowry to his house. So would men ne'er suffer ill at heaven's hand.

[**THETIS** vanishes.]

CHORUS [chanting]
Many are the shapes of Heaven's denizens, and many a thing they bring to pass contrary to our expectation; that which we thought would be is not accomplished, while for the unexpected God finds out a way. E'en such hath been the issue of this matter.

Euripides – A Short Biography

Euripides is rightly lauded as one of the great dramatists of all time. In his lifetime, he wrote over 90 plays and although only 18 have survived they reveal the scope and reach of his genius.

Euripides is identified with many theatrical innovations that have influenced drama all the way down to modern times, especially in the representation of traditional, mythical heroes as ordinary people in extraordinary circumstances. This new approach led him to pioneer developments that later writers would adapt to comedy. Yet he also became "the most tragic of poets", focusing on the inner lives and motives of his characters in a way previously unknown. He was "the creator of...that cage which is the theatre of Shakespeare's Othello, Racine's Phèdre, of Ibsen and Strindberg," in which "...imprisoned men and women destroy each other by the intensity of their loves and hates", and yet he was also the literary ancestor of comic dramatists as diverse as Menander and George Bernard Shaw.

As would be expected from a life lived 2,500 years ago, details of it are few and far between. Accounts of his life, written down the ages, do exist but whether much is reliable or surmised is open to debate.

Most accounts agree that he was born on Salamis Island around 480 BC, to mother Cleito and father Mnesarchus, a retailer who lived in a village near Athens. Upon the receipt of an oracle saying that his son was fated to win "crowns of victory", Mnesarchus insisted that the boy should train for a career in athletics.

His education was not only confined to athletics: he also studied painting and philosophy under the masters Prodicus and Anaxagoras.

However, what became quickly very clear was that athletics was not to be his way to win crowns of victory. Euripides had been lucky enough to have been born in the era as the other two masters of Greek Tragedy; Sophocles and Æschylus. It was in their footsteps that he was destined to follow.

His first play was performed some thirteen years after the first of Socrates plays and a mere three years after Æschylus had written his classic The Oristria.

Theatre was becoming a very important part of the Greek culture. The Dionysia, held annually, was the most important festival of theatre and second only to the fore-runner of the Olympic games, the

Panathenia, held every four years, in its appeal. It was a large festival in ancient Athens in honor of the god Dionysus, the central events of which were the theatrical performances of dramatic tragedies and, from 487 BC, comedies. The Dionysia actually consisted of two related festivals, the Rural Dionysia and the City Dionysia, which took place in different parts of the year.

Euripides first competed in the City Dionysia, in 455 BC, one year after the death of Æschylus, and, incredibly, it was not until 441 BC that he won first prize. His final competition in Athens was in 408 BC. However, The Bacchae and Iphigenia in Aulis were performed after his death in 405 BC and first prize was awarded posthumously. Altogether his plays won first prize only five times.

His plays, and those of Æschylus and Sophocles, indicate a difference in outlook between the three men, most easily explained as a generational gap, although with three great talents overlapping the driving forces may have pushed individual styles onwards perhaps faster than they may otherwise have done. Æschylus still looked back to the archaic period, Sophocles was in transition between periods, and Euripides was fully bonded with the new spirit of the classical age. When Euripides' plays are sequenced in time, they also show a developing pattern:

An early period of high tragedy (Medea, Hippolytus)
A patriotic period at the outset of the Peloponnesian War (Children of Hercules, Suppliants)
A middle period of disillusionment at the senselessness of war (Hecuba, Women of Troy)
An escapist period with a focus on romantic intrigue (Ion, Iphigenia in Tauris, Helen)
A final period of tragic despair (Orestes, Phoenician Women, Bacchae)

However, with over three quarters of his plays lost it is difficult to be certain as to whether the other works would also represent this development (e.g., Iphigenia at Aulis is dated with the 'despairing' Bacchae, yet it contains elements that became typical of New Comedy). In the Bacchae, he restores the chorus and messenger speech to their traditional role in the tragic plot, and the play appears to be the culmination of a regressive or archaizing tendency in his later works.

In one of his earliest surviving plays, Medea, includes a speech that he seems to have written in defence of himself as an intellectual ahead of his time, and to further challenge the times he has put the words in the mouth of the play's heroine:

"If you introduce new, intelligent ideas to fools, you will be thought frivolous, not intelligent. On the other hand, if you do get a reputation for surpassing those who are supposed to be intellectually sophisticated, you will seem to be a thorn in the city's flesh. This is what has happened to me." — Medea.

As we know Athenian tragedies during Euripides' lifetime were a public contest between playwrights. The state funded that contest and awarded prizes to the winners. The language was spoken and sung verse, the performance area included a circular floor or orchestra where the chorus could dance, a space for actors (usually three speaking actors in Euripides' time), a backdrop or skene and some special effects: an ekkyklema (used to bring the skene's "indoors" outdoors) and a mechane (used to lift actors in the air, as in deus ex machina). With the introduction of the third actor (an innovation attributed to Sophocles), acting also began to be regarded as a skill to be rewarded with prizes, requiring a long apprenticeship in the chorus. Euripides and other playwrights accordingly composed more and more arias for accomplished actors to sing and this tendency becomes more marked in his later plays: tragedy for him was a living and ever-changing genre.

Accounts by the famed comic poet, Aristophanes, characterise Euripides as a spokesman for destructive, new ideas, that mirror or help to bring about declining standards in both society and tragedy. However, 5th century tragedy was a social gathering for "carrying out quite publicly the maintenance and development of mental infrastructure" and it offered spectators a "platform for an utterly unique form of institutionalized discussion". A dramatist's role was not just to entertain but also to educate his fellow citizens—he was expected to have a message. Clearly this use of drama to democratize discussion was a very useful tool for all sides. Traditional myth provided the subject matter but the dramatist was meant to be innovative so as to sustain interest, which led to novel characterization of heroic figures and to use the mythical past to talk about present issues. The difference between Euripides and his older colleagues was, again, one of degree: his characters talked about the present more controversially and more pointedly than did those of Æschylus and Sophocles, sometimes even challenging the democratic order. Thus, for example, Odysseus is represented in Hecuba as "agile-minded, sweet-talking, demos-pleasing" i.e., a type of the war-time demagogues that were active in Athens during the Peloponnesian War. His concept is pleasingly simple. He retains the old stories and myths as well as the great names of the past and places them in the lives of contemporary Athenians thereby immediately help the audience understand it from the point of view of their own lives.

As mouthpieces for contemporary issues, they all seem to have had at least an elementary course in public speaking. Sometimes the dialogue often contrasts so strongly with the mythical and heroic setting, it looks as if Euripides aimed at parody, as for example in The Trojan Women, where the heroine's rationalized prayer provokes comment from Menelaus:

Hecuba:...O Zeus, whether you are the Law of Necessity in nature, or the Law of Reason in man, hear my prayers. You are everywhere, pursuing your noiseless path, ordering the affairs of mortals according to justice.

Menelaus: What's this? You are starting a new fashion in prayer.

Athenian citizens were familiar with rhetoric in the assembly and law courts, and some scholars believe that Euripides was more interested in his characters as speakers with cases to argue than as characters with lifelike personalities. They are self-conscious about speaking formally and their rhetoric is shown to be flawed, as if Euripides was exploring the problematical nature of language and communication: "For speech points in three different directions at once, to the speaker, to the person addressed, to the features in the world it describes, and each of these directions can be felt as skewed". Thus in the example above, Hecuba presents herself as a sophisticated intellectual describing a rationalised cosmos yet the speech is ill-matched to her audience, Menelaus (an unsophisticated listener), and soon it is found not to suit the cosmos either (her infant grandson is brutally murdered by the victorious Greeks).

Æschylus and Sophocles were innovative, but Euripides could move easily between tragic, comic, romantic and political effects, a versatility that appears in individual plays and also over the course of his career. Potential for comedy lay in his use of 'contemporary' characters, in his sophisticated tone, his relatively informal Greek, and his ingenious use of plots centered on motifs that later became standard, such as the 'recognition scene'. Other tragedians also used recognition scenes but they were heroic in emphasis, as in Æschylus's The Libation Bearers, which Euripides parodied with his mundane treatment of it in Electra (Euripides was unique among the tragedians in incorporating theatrical criticism in his plays). Traditional myth, with its exotic settings, heroic adventures and epic battles, offered potential for romantic melodrama as well as for political comments on a war theme, so that his plays are an extraordinary mix of elements. The Trojan Women for example is a powerfully disturbing play on the theme of war's horrors, apparently critical of Athenian imperialism (it was composed in the aftermath of the Melian massacre and during the preparations for the Sicilian Expedition) yet it features the comic exchange between Menelaus and Hecuba quoted above and the chorus considers Athens, the "blessed land of Theus", to be a desirable refuge—such complexity and ambiguity are typical both of his "patriotic" and "anti-war" plays.

Tragic poets in the 5th century competed against one another at the City Dionysia, each with a tetralogy consisting of three tragedies and a satyr-play. The few extant fragments of satyr-plays attributed to Æschylus and Sophocles indicate that these were a loosely structured, simple and jovial form of entertainment. However, in Cyclops (the only complete Euripides satyr-play that survives) the entertainment is structured more like a tragedy and introduced a note of critical irony typical of his other work. His genre-bending inventiveness is shown above all in Alcestis, a blend of tragic and satyric elements. This fourth play in his tetralogy for 438 BC (i.e., it occupied the position conventionally reserved for satyr-plays) is a "tragedy" that features Heracles as a satyric hero in conventional satyr-play scenes, involving an arrival, a banquet, a victory over an ogre (in this case, Death), a happy ending, a feast and a departure to new adventures.

Euripides was also a great lyric poet. In Medea, for example, he composed for his city, Athens, "the noblest of her songs of praise". His lyric skills however are not just confined to individual poems: "A play of Euripides is a musical whole....one song echoes motifs from the preceding song, while introducing new ones."

Much of his life and his whole career coincided with the struggle between Athens and Sparta for hegemony in Greece but he didn't live to see the final defeat of his city.

It is said that he died in Macedonia after being attacked by the Molossian hounds of King Archelaus and that his cenotaph near Piraeus was struck by lightning—signs of his unique powers, whether for good or ill. In an account by Plutarch, the complete failure of the Sicilian expedition led Athenians to trade renditions of Euripides' lyrics to their enemies in return for food and drink (Life of Nicias 29). Plutarch is the source also for the story that the victorious Spartan generals, having planned the demolition of Athens and the enslavement of its people, grew merciful after being entertained at a banquet by lyrics from Euripides' play Electra: "they felt that it would be a barbarous act to annihilate a city which produced such men" (Life of Lysander).

In The Frogs, composed after Euripides and Æschylus were both dead, Aristophanes imagines the god Dionysus venturing down to Hades in search of a good poet to bring back to Athens. After a debate between the two deceased bards, the god brings Æschylus back to life as more useful to Athens on account of his wisdom, rejecting Euripides as merely clever. Such comic 'evidence' suggests that Athenians admired Euripides even while they mistrusted his intellectualism, at least during the long war with Sparta.

Euripides had a famous library—one of the first to be privately collected. Although he lived most of his life in the midst of the cultured society of Athens, and was in some respects a leader in it, he grew bitter and despondent over the fierce rivalries and greedy ambitions which ran through the city. He loved the seclusion of his house at Salamis, where it was said that he composed his dramas in a cave.

Euripides fell out of favour with his fellow Athenian citizens and retired to the court of Archelaus, king of Macedon, who treated him with consideration and affection.

At his death, in around 406BC, he was mourned by the king, who, refusing the request of the Athenians that his remains be carried back to the Greek city, buried him with much splendor within his own dominions. His tomb was placed at the confluence of two streams, near Arethusa in Macedonia, and a cenotaph was built to his memory on the road from Athens towards the Piraeus.

Euripides – A Concise Bibliography

Alcestis (438 BC)
Medea (431 BC)
Heracleidae (c. 430 BC)
Hippolytus (428 BC)
Andromache (c. 425 BC)
Hecuba (c. 424 BC)
The Suppliants (c. 423 BC)
Electra (c. 420 BC)
Heracles (c. 416 BC)
The Trojan Women (c. 415 BC)
Iphigenia in Tauris (c. 414 BC)
Ion (c. 414 BC)
Helen (c. 412 BC)
Phoenician Women (c. 410 BC)
Orestes (c.408 BC)
Bacchae (405 BC)
Iphigenia at Aulis (405 BC)
Rhesus
Cyclops

Lost and Fragmentary Plays (Dated)

Peliades (455 BC)
Telephus (438 BC with Alcestis)
Alcmaeon in Psophis (438 BC with Alcestis)
Cretan Women (438 with Alcestis)
Cretans (c. 435 BC)
Philoctetes (431 BC with Medea)
Dictys (431 BC with Medea)
Theristai (satyr play, 431 BC with Medea)
Stheneboea (before 429 BC)
Bellerophon (c. 430 BC)
Cresphontes (ca. 425 BC)
Erechtheus (422 BC)
Phaethon (c. 420 BC)

Wise Melanippe (c. 420 BC)
Alexandros (415 BC with Trojan Women)
Palamedes (415 BC with Trojan Women)
Sisyphus (satyr play, 415 BC with Trojan Women)
Captive Melanippe (c. 412 BC)
Andromeda (412 BC with Helen)
Antiope (c. 410 BC)
Archelaus (c. 410 BC)
Hypsipyle (c. 410 BC)
Alcmaeon in Corinth (c. 405 BC) Won first prize as part of a trilogy with The Bacchae and Iphigenia in Aulis.

Lost and Fragmentary Plays (Not Dated)

Aegeus
Aeolus
Alcmene
Alope, or Cercyon
Antigone
Auge
Autolycus
Busiris
Cadmus
Chrysippus
Danae
Epeius
Eurystheus
Hippolytus Veiled
Ino
Ixion
Lamia
Licymnius
Meleager
Mysians
Oedipus
Oeneus
Oenomaus
Peirithous
Peleus
Phoenix
Phrixus
Pleisthenes
Polyidus
Protesilaus
Reapers
Rhadamanthys
Sciron